Daniel and the Whale Hunters

Far off the coast of Portugal lie the Azores islands, where men still hunt whales with hand harpoons. This dangerous pursuit is a sure challenge to adventurous boys — such as Daniel Martiniano, of the island of Pico.

After years of waiting, Daniel has finally been promised the chance to go whale hunting with his father. But until the whales are sighted, he and his family have much other work to do . . . farming the stony island fields, baking, caring for whaling equipment, preparing for a festival. Then at last the whales come, and Daniel goes to sea with the brave whalers of Pico.

Here, in words and superb photographs, is an exciting account of Daniel's first whale hunt — and an intriguing portrait of another way of life.

Bernard Wolf, a free-lance photographer, spent weeks in the Azores taking pictures for this book — and waiting just as impatiently as Daniel for the arrival of the whales. Mr. Wolf has written and photographed two other children's books about life in other lands: *The Little Weaver of Agato* and *Jamaica Boy*.

Daniel and the Whale Hunters

The adventures of a Portuguese boy in a whaling town in the Azores
written and photographed by Bernard Wolf

Random House New York

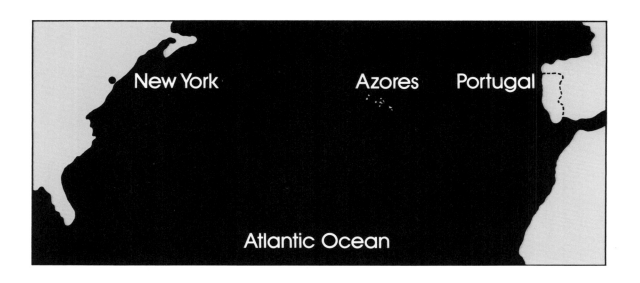

New York   Azores   Portugal

Atlantic Ocean

This book is dedicated to the Martiniano family
and to the brave whalers of Lajes do Pico.
Boa fortuna!

For their generous help during the preparation of this book, the author is grateful to Architect Carlos Lemeiro, Director, and Commander José Cabral, Counsellor on Tourism, both of Casa da Portugal, New York City; to Evelyn Heyward Associates, New York City and Lisbon; and especially to Senhora Olga Avila, Senhor Ermelindo Avila, and their son Paul Luis Avila, of the island of Pico.

Library of Congress Cataloging in Publication Data. Wolf, Bernard. Daniel and the whale hunters. SUMMARY: Text and photographs introduce the life of a Portuguese boy from a whaling village in the Azores. 1. Children in the Azores—Juvenile literature. 2. Pico (Island)—Social life and customs—Juvenile literature. 3. Whaling—Pico (Island)—Juvenile literature. [1. Children in the Azores. 2. Pico (Island)—Social life and customs. 3. Whaling—Pico (Island)] I. Title.
DP702.A95W64 914.69'9 75-37417 ISBN 0-394-82359-1 ISBN 0-394-92359-6 (lib. bdg.)

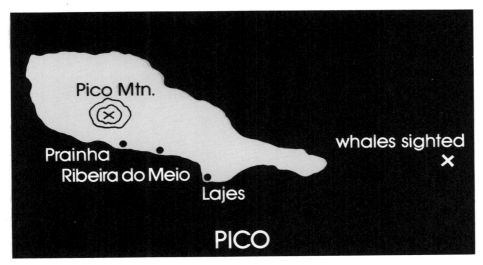

Pico Mtn.

Prainha
Ribeira do Meio
Lajes

whales sighted
✕

PICO

The Azores Archipelago consists of nine tiny, volcanically formed islands in the Atlantic Ocean. They were discovered and claimed by Portuguese explorers in the fifteenth century. Today the inhabitants of these islands are citizens of Portugal.

The island of Pico is the sixth island of the archipelago. It is dominated by a spectacular volcanic mountain that soars to a height of 7,611 feet. The men of Pico are considered to be the best sailors and fishermen in the Azores. Their island has also been called the island of the whale hunters.

It is six-thirty on a Saturday morning on the island of Pico. Daniel Francisco Vieira Martiniano is riding his uncle's horse up the hillside above the town of Lajes. Attached to the saddle is a tin milk pail, for Daniel is on his way to milk the family cow. He enjoys doing this, but today he is thinking of other things.

"When will the whales come, Rosalia?" he asks the horse as he pulls her to a halt and looks out to sea.

It is only the beginning of May—still early in the season for whaling. But Daniel is impatient. In the distance he can see old Pico Mountain, with scarcely any haze covering the top.

"If the weather continues so clear, the *baleia* will never come," he says with disgust.

Daniel is fifteen years old. For three years he has pleaded with his father, Francisco, to take him on a whale hunt. But Francisco has always refused.

"It is dangerous enough for an ex-perienced whaler, let alone a young boy," his father has explained. "Besides, Daniel, you know that every man in my crew would be personally responsible for your safety. That's a lot to ask of them. No, no. You must wait awhile."

But this year, at long last, Francisco has given his permission, and Captain Soares and the rest of the crew have agreed. Of course Daniel won't be allowed in the whaling boat itself. He will have to go in the motor launch, but still—

"Just think, Rosalia. It's finally going to happen!"

Rosalia continues calmly up the path. The hill they are climbing is covered with narrow, terraced fields. These have been dug out of the cliffside, one above the other, by centuries of back-breaking toil. Above them the land is flatter, though still rugged. Most of the farming is done here along the coast-line, since the island's interior is rocky and mountainous.

After climbing for twenty minutes, Daniel and Rosalia reach the high pasture where Vermelha, the milk cow, is grazing. The pasture is a small field used only for the cow and a few goats. It is fenced in by a wall of lava rocks piled loosely on top of one another.

Daniel jumps to the ground and tethers the horse. He gathers some fresh ferns for Vermelha, and while she munches on them, he milks her.

When the pail is full, Daniel has his breakfast. He eats some bread that he has brought with him, and to wash it down, he drinks some *really* fresh milk.

Daniel remounts Rosalia by stepping on the milk can and heaving himself into the saddle. Once seated, he lifts the full can of milk up by a rope.

Daniel is small for his age and this sometimes bothers him. But his father has told him, "Listen, Daniel, when I was your age, I was no taller. Size isn't important if you want to be a whaler. You need strength, courage, quick wits, and patience. Right now," Francisco added with a smile, "you could use a little more patience! But don't worry. One day you'll be an even better whaler than I am."

9

Daniel hurries back down to Lajes and gives the milk to his mother. Before beginning his day's work, he is going to see Senhor (Mr.) Baretto at the whaling lookout post, and he is eager to be off.

The lookout post is a small concrete hut on top of a cliff overlooking the sea. From early spring until the end of the whaling season in the fall, someone is always on duty during the daylight hours. Each of the whalers in the area takes his turn as lookout, carefully scanning the water with high-powered binoculars.

"*Bom dia!* Good morning, Senhor Baretto! Have you seen any whales yet?" Daniel calls as he arrives.

"*Bom dia,* Daniel. You really are getting impatient, aren't you? No, no whales yet. It's still a little early in the season," replies the whaler. "Besides, we've had nothing but good weather lately. You know the whales won't come close to land unless a storm at sea drives them in to calmer waters."

Senhor Baretto notices Daniel's eager gaze on the binoculars and laughs. "Here, Daniel. You take a look. Who knows? Maybe you'll have better luck."

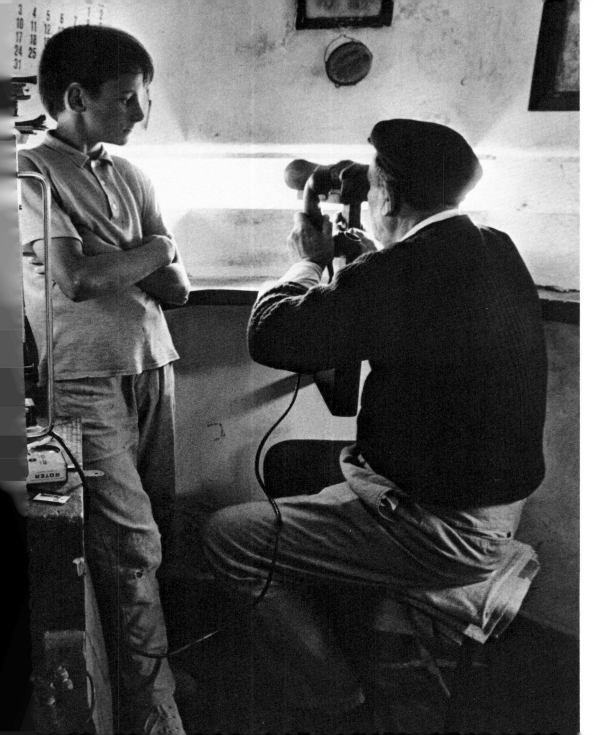

Daniel quickly looks through the instrument. "Nothing but a lot of water," he mutters after a moment.

"Exactly!" says Baretto with a grin.

He shows Daniel a chart of the sea surrounding the area, pointing out the places where whales have been sighted before and are likely to reappear.

When whales are sighted, the lookout sets off rockets to alert the town. Every whaler within earshot drops whatever he is doing and runs for his boat.

Only the whaler on lookout duty remains on shore, to work the radio telephone transmitter in the post. Throughout the hunt, he radios the precise location of the whales to the captains of the motor launches.

"And now, Daniel," says Baretto, "if you want me to find some whales, I'd better get back to looking for them. Don't be discouraged. They may appear any day. Just keep your ears tuned for the rockets."

Today Daniel has been hired to work on the field of a townsman. For this he is paid the same wages as a grown man: 50 escudos a day without lunch or 45 escudos a day with wine and lunch. An escudo is worth about 3½ cents in United States currency.

Daniel helps to prepare the soil for a new planting by spreading *boana* on the earth. *Boana* is a rich fertilizer made from the ground bones of whales.

Daniel has completed grammar school, but only just barely. He has no patience for books. Instead, he enjoys using his wits and his hands for practical purposes.

He is constantly looking for any work he can get. In a good week during the spring and summer months, he may find two or three days of paid work. He gives whatever money he earns to his father to help support the family. So does his 19-year-old brother, José Manuel, who is an apprentice mason.

Daniel's mother is called Maria do Egipto, which means Mary of Egypt. She is a gentle woman who rarely raises her voice in anger and never complains about life's hardships.

This will be an especially busy day for Maria do Egipto because she is going to bake a two weeks' supply of *bolo,* bread made from ground corn. What with all the excitement of the *festas* (festivals) that will take place next week, there won't be time for baking then.

She has invited two neighbors to share her large oven for baking their own *bolo.* A roaring wood fire is preheating the oven. The women pour the ingredients for the dough into a tub of boiling water. Using a long wooden spoon, Maria do Egipto stirs the mixture into a rich, creamy dough.

Next she shapes the dough into large balls. Then each ball is patted into a flat, round shape. This must be done quickly before the dough can cool and harden.

14

Now the *bolo* is ready to be baked. Using a broom made of fresh ferns, one of the neighbors sweeps the hot oven free of ashes and wood. Maria do Egipto puts the *bolo* into the oven with a long wooden paddle. When the bread is baked, she sets it on a bundle of twigs to cool.

Only a few weeks ago Maria do Egipto's father died. Now she is in mourning. She will dress in black for one year, as is customary in respect for the death of a parent or a brother or sister. Had one of her own children died or her husband, she would wear black for the rest of her life.

Maria do Egipto's eldest daughter, 13-year-old Nisalda, has been washing the floor in the front room during the baking.

Nisalda is cleaning the house for her father's return from Faial, a nearby island. Francisco went to the island yesterday to buy a pig and to help Captain Soares repair the radio telephone of his whaling motor launch.

Late in the afternoon, Nisalda walks down to the small pier at the town's waterfront and arrives just as Francisco gets off the launch.

"Bem vindo, Pai! Welcome back, Father!" cries Nisalda with delight.

Francisco greets her with a hug. "Just look at this crazy pig," he says. "What a rotten sailor he is! Imagine— only a short boat ride and already he's seasick!"

Francisco keeps a tight hold on the unsteady pig. With his free hand, he opens a basket and shows Nisalda the small gifts he has bought for each member of the family. "You see," he adds with a grin, "I've even bought a present for myself—a bottle of brandy!"

Nisalda repacks the basket and places it on her head. As they walk back along the waterfront, Francisco's friends call out greetings to him.

When they arrive at the house, Francisco is surrounded by his family. Everyone starts trying to hug him and ask questions at the same time. Then Daniel feeds some corn to the pig and the rest of the family gather around to admire it.

The pig cost 500 escudos—a lot of money. But after it is fattened and slaughtered, it will provide the family with lard, sausages, and meat for the next five or six months. Francisco usually buys two pigs each year and, if the whaling is good, sometimes three.

Francisco Adelino Vieira Martiniano is a small man, but he possesses tremendous energy and strength. He has known hard work all his life. He has much to be proud of: the love of a wonderful family, the respect of his fellow townsmen and whalers, and the sure knowledge of his own capabilities. Whaling is a way of life for him as it was for his father, a great whaling harpooner, and for his forefathers back to the eighteenth century.

The next day, Sunday, Francisco and the family attend morning Mass. After lunch, Daniel is free to do what he likes. He spends the rest of the day playing soccer with his friends.

As the boys separate to go home for dinner, Daniel looks up at the sky. There are low, heavy clouds and strong gusts of wind. Pico Mountain is completely obscured. Who knows? Perhaps tomorrow the whales will come.

When Daniel awakens the next day, he rushes out of bed to examine the weather. The sun is shining brilliantly and there isn't a cloud to be seen. Sighing, he gets dressed.

This morning Daniel will help his father plant corn in one of Francisco's fields. Francisco has already gone on ahead. Daniel has time for only a cup of coffee and a piece of bread for breakfast. Then he rushes off, carrying a basket of lunch, a sickle, and some light clothing to change into when the day gets warmer.

He climbs for forty minutes to his father's field. When he arrives, he finds Francisco and a friend, Jorge Alves Moniz, hard at work. Daniel relieves his father behind the wood plow. It takes a lot of strength to plow a straight furrow across the field, but Daniel enjoys the challenge. As he puts all of his energy into the job, he keeps up a steady conversation with the cattle that pull the plow, joking and calling out to each of them by name.

Jorge follows Daniel, sprinkling kernels of corn into the freshly plowed furrows and laughing at Daniel's comments.

Francisco is hard at work at the edge of the field, hacking away at the weeds and rocks that clog the earth. Every inch of soil must be used.

It's a good feeling to have one's own land. Francisco's family will never go hungry while he has his strength and skill as a farmer. Still, life is a constant struggle for survival. Francisco's fields produce just enough for his family's needs. There is never anything left over to be sold. Occasionally Francisco may sell a cow or a goat, but most of the cash he earns during the year comes from whaling.

By noon, work on the field is finished and it's time for lunch. Francisco opens the lunch basket and takes out a loaf of fresh *bolo,* cheese, sausage, and delicious omelettes. There is also a can of hot coffee. The three men have worked up huge appetites and eat everything.

After lunch, Francisco and Jorge go off to prepare one of Jorge's fields for planting. By helping each other, both men avoid having to pay a fieldhand.

Daniel has found a few hours of paid work on one of the townsmen's fields this afternoon, and he hurries away.

Maria do Egipto is busy ironing a huge laundry which she started yesterday. She is getting all of the family's best clothing ready for the *festas,* which begin tomorrow. At her side is 4-year-old Humberta, her youngest daughter.

Outside the family's third daughter, Noelia, engages in her favorite sport of teasing the chickens. Noelia is a high-spirited girl of six who can never sit still for a moment. She isn't afraid of anything—except possibly one large rooster, who always pecks her when she enters the chicken coop.

"You'd better watch out, you big monster," she taunts him from behind the safety of the wire fence, "because I'm coming in anyway!"

In a flash she slips into the coop with a big stick to protect herself. When the rooster makes a diving peck at her leg, Noelia backs away, shaking her stick wrathfully.

"You just wait," she scolds him. "I'll get you yet. Just wait!"

Maria do Egipto finishes her ironing and can rest for a while. Hearing a racket from the chicken coop, she calls to Noelia to come out and leave the poor chickens alone.

"Come and sit by my side, Noelia," she says, seating Humberta on her lap. "Now listen to me, both of you, and listen well. I'm going to tell you a wonderful, true story about the giving of vesper bread."

The girls settle down expectantly. Maria do Egipto is a good storyteller and they always enjoy listening to her tales.

"Once upon a time, long, long ago," she begins, "there lived in the Kingdom of Portugal a very beautiful queen named Isabel and a very brave warrior king called Dinis the Fearful."

"Were they married?" asks Noelia.

"Naturally, they were married," replies Maria do Egipto patiently. "Now, King Dinis was called 'the Fearful' because he had killed many enemies while defending Portugal. His subjects knew that he was a good king, but they were afraid to look at his face because he appeared so fierce and cruel.

"The times were very hard in Portugal then. Many people were starving because King Dinis had to spend so much money for wars.

"Queen Isabel's heart was moved by the suffering in her kingdom. Whenever she could, she gave food to the poor — sometimes, even her own food.

"'How can you give food away?' her husband would shout with rage. 'We scarcely have enough to eat ourselves. You must never do it again!'

"One day, King Dinis went off with some of his soldiers to inspect his fortresses. While he was gone, Queen Isabel ordered her kitchen staff to bake many loaves of bread. As soon as they were out of the oven, she put them all in her skirts and hurried down the road to give them to the poor.

"Suddenly, she saw her husband riding toward her with a furious expression on his face!

"'What are you carrying in your skirts, my lady?' asked the king.

"Isabel was terrified. Turning her face to heaven, she prayed with all her soul for a miracle. After a long moment, she looked at her husband and calmly replied, 'Why, flowers, my lord,' and with her heart in her mouth, she lowered her skirts to the ground. Lo and behold! Out fell a glowing mound of beautiful roses!"

Humberta laughs with delight but Noelia looks skeptical.

"And that is why, each year, we observe the custom of giving vesper bread during the Festival of the Holy Spirit," concludes Maria do Egipto. "You will see this for yourselves when we go to the *festas.*"

"Well, I suppose it *was* a miracle," concedes Noelia after a long moment of thought. But Maria do Egipto doesn't hear her. She has gone back to work in the kitchen.

Late that afternoon Daniel arrives home from the fields. He is pleased to find his grandmother there, taking charge of the house while Maria do

Egipto is out shopping. With her is her great-grandnephew, whom she is looking after for the day.

"*Boa tarde,* Daniel! Good afternoon!" his grandmother greets him heartily. "I have a real treat for you today," she says with a wink. "Before your mother went out, she left strict instructions that you are to wash your hair and have it cut this evening."

Daniel groans and mutters, but finally resigns himself to his fate. He rolls back his collar and is soon scrubbing his head energetically and exchanging teasing remarks with his grandmother.

31

Meanwhile, Francisco returns home through the streets of Lajes and finds Daniel just rinsing out his hair.

"O, Daniel, I hear Joachim Machado is eager to give you a haircut," Francisco teases his son. Joachim Machado, the town's barber, is also the captain of Francisco's whaling boat.

"By the way," Francisco continues casually, "I just spoke to Machado and a few of my other crewmates. We've all agreed that it's time to start teaching you about our whaling boat. So, if you can spare the time after your haircut, I'll pick you up at the barbershop and we'll all meet down at the whaling boat shed. Of course, if there are other things you would rather do—"

"Oh, no, no, no, *Pai*!" exclaims Daniel excitedly. "I'm leaving this second!"

33

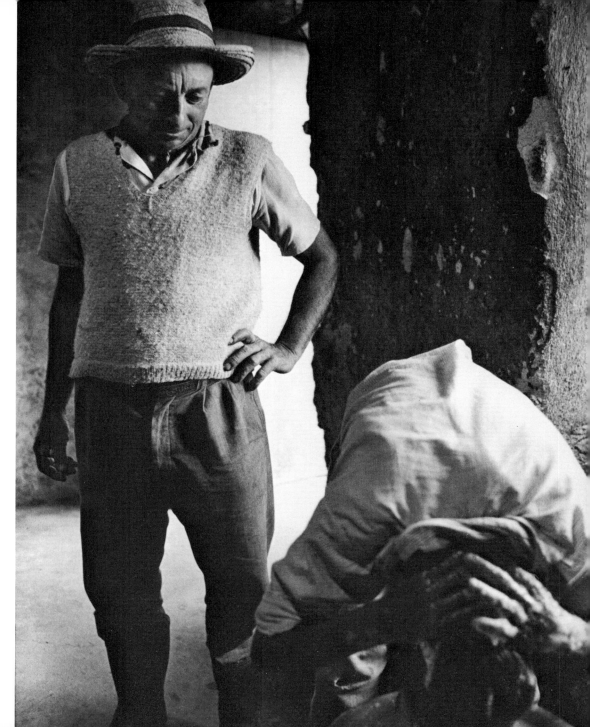

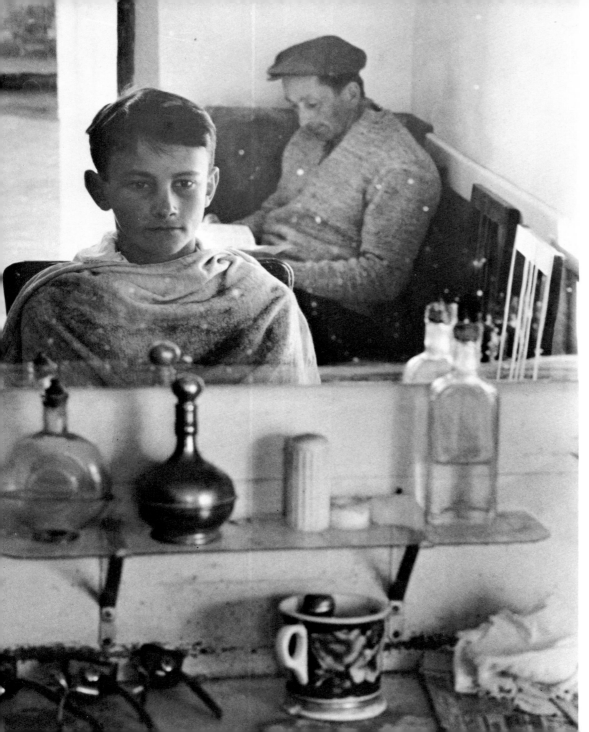

Daniel can scarcely sit still for his haircut. All his life he has watched the whaling boats go to sea, but he has only a general idea of how they work. Never before have the whalers offered to teach him about their jobs. As soon as the barber finishes, Daniel hurries him and Francisco toward the boat shed.

The three whaling boats of Lajes are kept in separate sheds on the shallower part of the waterfront, about three hundred feet from the town's pier. There are also three motor launches, one to tow each whale boat. These ride at anchor off the tip of the pier, where the water is deeper. The whale boats, sheds, motor launches, and the equipment that they contain are all owned by the Whaling Association of Lajes do Pico.

When Daniel, Francisco, and Machado arrive, they find José Vigario, the boat's harpooner, waiting for them.

"Here comes our star pupil!" Vigario booms out.

Joachim Machado unlocks a large, heavy padlock, and the men swing the thick wooden doors of the boat shed open. There, gleaming richly in a new coat of paint, sits the whale boat!

It is a small but beautiful craft, measuring about thirty-six feet in length by six feet in width. Its sleek lines give it maximum speed.

The boat is specially designed for whaling. At the beginning of the hunt, it is towed into open water by a motor launch. When a whale is sighted, the boat can be easily converted into a sailboat. This allows the crew to approach the whale quickly and quietly. As they get close to the animal, they take down the sails and bring out oars. The craft becomes a rowboat, giving the men more control over its movements.

Machado tells Daniel how the men divide their work and take care of the boat. "In the whaling season," he concludes, "we must keep the boat and everything in it in perfect condition all the time. An oversight could cost us our lives."

Machado is not joking. As captain of his boat, he is responsible for the life of each member of his crew. The boat's crew consists of the captain, the harpooner, four oarsmen, and one man who assists the captain and the harpooner. This last job is Francisco's.

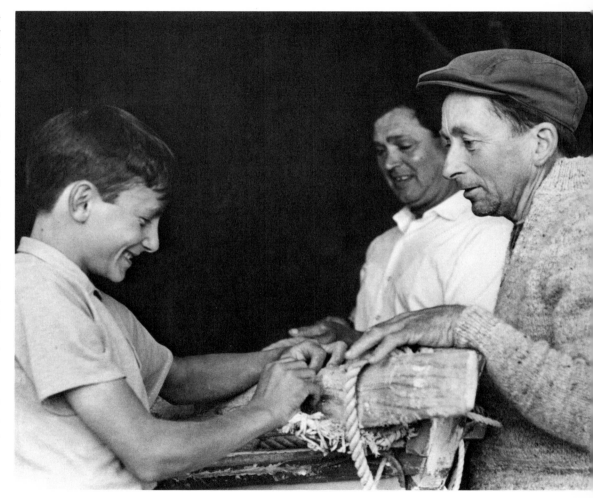

"And now, Daniel," challenges José Vigario "let's test your strength. Our first task when we go for whales is to pull the boat out of the shed and get her into the water as quickly as possible. Let's see if you can move her a little bit with our help."

The whale boat rests on thick wood blocks. On each one, a deep chunk has been carved out of the upper surface. When the boat is pulled out of the shed, additional blocks are placed on the paving to make a guide rail running down to the edge of the water.

Daniel and the men take positions around the boat. On Machado's count of three, Daniel pushes with all his might. The boat doesn't budge.

On the fourth attempt the boat finally moves forward—about three inches.

"Not bad, not bad," says Francisco. "Of course, this isn't a fair test. It really takes seven strong men to move the boat into the water."

"Tell me, *Pai,* when will I be allowed to go out in the whale boat?" asks Daniel eagerly.

"Not so fast, Daniel," says the harpooner. "You must learn to float before you can swim. First you will ride in the motor launch. Besides, it isn't wise for a father and son to be in the same whale boat together. What would happen to your family if you were both injured or killed? It has happened before. Why, it almost happened to Francisco, here, once when he went out whaling in the same boat with your grandfather, Manuel Martiniano."

Although Daniel has heard this tale many times before, he never tires of it. He listens intently as the harpooner recalls how Francisco was once knocked into the water when a wounded whale brushed against his boat. The whale then surfaced alongside Francisco, crushing him against the side of the craft.

"It all happened so quickly the men could hardly believe it," Vigario goes on. "But in a flash, your grandfather placed his shoulder against the side of the whale. With every vein standing out on his face, he slowly forced the boat away from the whale, while with his right hand, he grabbed Francisco by the collar and hauled him on board. What a man your grandfather was," the harpooner concludes in awe. The other men nod their heads in agreement.

Machado finally breaks the silence. "And now, gentlemen, I must return to my shop. Daniel, if you have more questions, why don't you see Senhor Soares, Jr.? I'm sure he'd be pleased to tell you all you want to know."

Manuel Viera Soares, Jr. is an unusual and brave man. For most of his life, he has suffered from crippling arthritis. As a youth, his ambition was to become a whaler, but because of his affliction, this was impossible. By sheer will power, he slowly regained the partial use of his legs and the full use of his hands. He began to build precise scale models of whaling boats and discovered that he had a great talent for this work. Today, his model boats are in museums around the world.

Daniel stops by the model maker's on the way home. Soares greets him warmly and listens with interest to Daniel's account of the lesson at the boat shed. Then he brings out a beautiful scale model of a whaling boat with its mast and sails raised. It is a remarkable piece of craftsmanship, accurate in every detail. The model includes miniature replicas of every piece of equipment that would be found on a working whale boat.

"You know, Daniel," says Senhor Soares, "these whaling boats were introduced to Pico by the whalers of New Bedford, Massachusetts, in the early nineteenth century. Very little in our methods has changed since then. The New Bedford whalers were very skillful men."

Senhor Soares points out various items on the boat and explains their use to Daniel. Harpoons, lances, rope, oars, an axe, drinking water, signal flags—the list goes on and on.

Daniel wonders how he will ever remember everything. Whaling is much more complicated than he thought.

The following morning, while Maria do Egipto is busy bathing and dressing the children for the *festas,* there is a sudden explosion outside.

"What's that?" exclaims Daniel.

"Oh, they're just setting off some fireworks to celebrate the *festas,*" replies his mother calmly.

But then, there is another explosion even closer by—SHH-CRACK!—and after a hushed silence, a cry rings out: *"BA-LEI-A!"*

Daniel rushes to the door and flings it open, listening hard.

Another rocket goes off and again the cry *"BA-LEI-A!"* There is no mistake. The whales have come at last!

"I must get to the motor launch, *Mãe,*" Daniel calls to his mother. He stops long enough to grab some food and his windbreaker, then dashes out of the house toward the waterfront.

Francisco is up in the cow pasture above the town. When he hears the rockets, he takes off down the cliff like a mountain goat! His feet barely seem to touch the ground as he vaults over stone walls and other obstacles in his path.

Daniel reaches the end of the pier just as Captain Soares begins to start up the engine of his motor launch, the *Cigana* (Gypsy).

"Jump on board quickly, and keep out of the way, Daniel," he says. "We have no time to lose."

As Daniel obeys, the burly captain casts off from the pier and slowly edges the launch out into deeper water.

Meanwhile, along the town's waterfront, men are converging from all directions upon the whaling boat sheds. Francisco suddenly appears with his crewmates. The doors of their shed are quickly unlocked and pulled open. The guide blocks are placed in position as the men rush to both sides of the boat.

This is a serious race. The first boat that gets away will not only have the best chance for a kill, but will also be given the teeth of the first whale killed. Whale teeth can be sold for as much as sixty escudos per pound.

Francisco and his crew put their shoulders to the whale boat and heave mightily. In just four minutes, the boat is in the water and the crew has boarded her. The men begin to row powerfully toward the deeper water where the *Cigana* is waiting.

As the boat approaches the motor launch, the oars are pulled back and stowed on board. The men quickly remove their shoes. From now until the end of their hunt, they will remain barefooted in order to have a better grip on the slippery surfaces of the boat.

"Ahoy, you lazy fellows! What took you so long?" shouts Captain Soares as he throws a heavy rope from the launch to the boat.

José Vigario, standing at the prow of his boat, deftly catches it. "What are you complaining about?" he yells back, laughing. "We're the first ones out, aren't we?"

While Vigario fastens the line to the whale boat, Francisco carefully checks that everything is in its proper place. Satisfied with his inspection, he raises his hand and waves at Soares.

"All right. Let's go!" he calls.

The men settle down. Soares opens the throttle of his engine to full power, and with a tremendous roar the hunt is on!

The motor launch tows the whale boat at top speed, keeping fairly close to the shoreline of Pico Island. Francisco sits at the tiller in the stern guiding the whale boat past rocks.

It is perfect weather for whaling. The skies are heavily overcast, and there is a brisk wind with occasional light showers. The waters are fairly calm here, but undoubtedly a large storm is raging farther out in the Atlantic.

About an hour and a half later, the two boats clear the last rocky outcropping of the southeasternmost point of Pico. Daniel finds himself a comfortable seat on a coil of rope on the rear deck of the motor launch. From here he has a fine view of his father's boat, and he can easily see in all directions. As the launch heads out toward the open sea, Daniel begins to feel more and more excited.

They are seventeen miles at sea when Francisco looks over his shoulder to find a second whale boat bearing down upon them. He turns over control of the tiller to Joachim Machado and leaps to the prow of the boat, where he stands anxiously scanning the horizon.

"*BA-LEI-A!*" cries out Francisco. His sharp eyes are the first to spot the whales. At a great distance, he can just make out their shapes and the spouts of water they are throwing into the air through their blowholes.

44

Soares, on the motor launch, hears Francisco and immediately gets on his radio telephone.

"Attention! Attention! *Cigana* calling the lookout post. Captain Soares speaking. We have made contact with the whales but we are not sure how many there are. What is your count? Do you read me? Over."

A voice crackles through the wire. "I read you and can see you clearly. I make five whales."

Soares swings the launch toward the whales. Francisco and his crew have already raised their boat's mast and are making fast the lines for the sails.

Captain Soares cuts his engine back to half power, still towing the whale boat.

Moving with split-second coordination, the whalers unfurl the sails, attach them to the mast, and start hoisting them up.

At the bow, José Vigario casts off the line from the motor launch. The sails are set.

Captain Soares reduces his engine to a low murmur in order not to alarm the whales.

The whale boat is now on its own. What a brave sight it makes as it sails off alone in pursuit of its quarry!

With the aid of a good, steady wind, the whale boat is soon close to the whales. Now the men quickly lower the sails and take down the mast. They remove the rudder and replace it with a long steering oar, which Machado takes control of. Instructions are given in hoarse whispers as the oarsmen bring out their oars. They pull the boat as quietly as possible up to the whale that José Vigario has selected as their target.

48

Daniel almost yells a warning from the motor launch. The whale boat is now barely three feet from the animal's back! If it touches the whale, it will scare the animal off.

Machado, holding the steering oar, urgently signals the men to stop the boat. At the prow, José Vigario stands cooly poised with his harpoon held ready. Behind him stands Francisco, who holds the line attached to the harpoon, ready to play it out.

Vigario carefully braces himself, slowly raises the harpoon over his head, takes aim, and with a great heave launches it into the back of the whale's head. He has made the first strike and it is a good one!

For a stunned moment the whale remains still, unable to understand what has happened to it. Then, with a vast shudder and without warning, the animal dives headfirst into the sea.

"Look out, *Pai!*" screams Daniel.

This is the most dangerous moment of the hunt, for no one can predict exactly when the whale will dive or where it will surface. But Francisco and the members of his crew know their jobs well. The oarsmen immediately row the boat out of reach of the whale's swinging tail. Francisco helps the rope attached to the harpoon unwind from its tub without catching on anything— especially himself. The rope unwinds very quickly. It would catch fire from friction if one of the oarsmen did not constantly water the spot where it rubs against the boat's bulwarks.

The whale can remain underwater for only about twenty minutes before it is forced to the surface for air. But sometimes, in its frantic efforts to dislodge the harpoon from its flesh, a whale will tow a boat out to sea for many hours. Today the whalers are in luck. The whale surfaces after only ten minutes, at a safe distance, and stays put.

Francisco hauls in the harpoon line and rewinds it as the oarsmen row up to the whale once again.

José Vigario determines that the harpoon is securely placed. Therefore a second harpoon will not be required. Francisco hands him a lance to which a shorter and thinner line is attached. Unlike the barbed end of a harpoon, the lance has a clean cutting edge.

Once again, Vigario stands ready at the boat's prow. With another powerful heave, the lance finds its mark close to the point where the harpoon lies fixed. Again, the oarsmen row the boat away from the whale. Francisco tugs at the line attached to the lance and retrieves the weapon. Vigario has inflicted a deep wound but, surprisingly, the whale does not move. A dark, red stain slowly begins to discolor the surface of the water.

Captain Soares gently eases the motor launch closer to the whale boat.

After witnessing the second successful strike, Daniel feels a bit more reassured. But still, he can't help thinking how defenseless the tiny boat and the men in it appear against the mighty bulk of the whale. Francisco's boat has harpooned a 45-foot sperm whale. For the first time, Daniel fully realizes how easily the whalers could be destroyed by this giant.

José Vigario has thrown lance after lance and the whale has dived twice more. The sea is stained dull red now. The beast is exhausted and mortally wounded but still not dead.

As captain of his boat, it is up to Machado to deliver the final blow. Exchanging places with Vigario, he takes the lance, studies his target thoughtfully, and drives home a long, deep thrust. A faint tremor runs through the animal's long body. Then, nothing. The whale is dead.

While the oarsmen hold the boat steady, Francisco picks up the long cutting spade and chops a hole through the whale's tail. Then two of the other men pass a heavy hauling line through the hole and tie it tightly.

The *Cigana* moves up alongside the dead whale. Captain Soares turns the steering wheel over to his engineer and runs to the rail of the launch. Francisco throws the end of the hauling line to him and Soares fastens it loosely to the rail.

Then, with the aid of a grappling pole, Soares steadies the whale against the side of the launch while one of the whalers plants a red flag in the animal's body.

"Not bad for a start," says Soares.

All at once Daniel becomes aware that he is freezing and very hungry. He quickly puts on his windbreaker and starts munching on some bread and cheese. As he eats, he studies the enormous whale lying in the water.

A second whale has been sighted nearby! Machado tells Soares that they are going after it and the captain agrees, though he doesn't like the look of the weather. Heavy, black clouds are beginning to move in their direction. In the distance the muffled sound of thunder can be heard. Soares wouldn't care to be caught out here in a storm — especially not with two whales in tow.

Soares casts off the hauling line attached to the whale and returns to the launch's cockpit. The dead whale with its red flag will be left to float and can easily be picked up later on.

The oarsmen row the whale boat as swiftly as possible to their new prey, about 150 yards off.

José Vigario stands ready with his harpoon. He throws, but the weapon is deflected by a muscle in the whale's back and falls off into the water. The startled animal advances upon the boat, rocking the craft as he comes!

"Quickly! Quickly!" shouts Machado, throwing all his weight on the steering oar in a desperate attempt to turn the boat aside.

At the same instant, both Francisco and the harpooner fling themselves on the oars nearest to them. With a tremendous heave, they just barely manage to avoid a collision with the onrushing beast. The whale churns past them like a huge, black torpedo. It finally comes to a halt about sixty feet away, still on the surface.

"Give me that!" says Vigario fiercely, grabbing the harpoon which Francisco has just fished from the sea. "This time, there will be no mistakes!"

Once again the boat approaches the whale. Vigario musters every ounce of his strength and launches his harpoon deep into the animal's side. Immediately a torrent of blood gushes into the air from its blowhole. The men hastily row the boat away.

But the whale does not dive. Vigario has punctured one of its lungs, and it now needs all the air it can get.

The oarsmen cautiously row up the boat and José Vigario poises his lance for a second strike.

Within an hour, the whale has been killed.

While Francisco's crew and Captain Soares attach hauling lines between the dead whales and fasten them to the motor launch, the two other launches from Lajes slowly come up alongside the *Cigana.*

"No luck, eh, Joao?" calls Soares to another captain.

"Bah!" the man snorts in disgust. "What can you expect from a bunch of old women?"

As consolation, Soares offers to buy the other captain some wine when they get back to Lajes. The captain accepts and, opening the throttle of his engine, he roars off. Behind his launch he tows the two unlucky whaling boats.

Now the third motor launch approaches Francisco's whale boat. The engineer throws a tow line to José Vigario. As the launch gets under way, the engineer calls out, "Oh, Francisco! Your wife brought this sweater to the pier this morning just after you left. Here, catch!"

The man throws the sweater to Francisco but his aim is poor. The sweater lands in the sea as the whale boat sweeps past.

"Stop! Stop, you damned fools!"

shouts Francisco, shaking his fist at the launch. But his voice can't be heard above the sound of the engine. None of his crewmates laugh. A heavy woolen sweater is expensive. Besides, it will be a long, cold haul back to Lajes in the open boat.

Francisco furiously throws off the towing line. Then he grabs a pair of oars, rows back to where the sweater is floating, and fishes it out of the water.

The motor launch turns back to pick up Francisco's boat once more. As the towing line is refastened, the men huddle down for the return trip to Lajes.

Because of the weight of the whales that she is towing, the *Cigana* will reach Lajes late at night, long after the whale boats have returned. Captain Soares will leave the whales on the waterfront below the whale processing factory, on the outskirts of Lajes.

"Well, Daniel, what do you think? Do you still want to become a whaler?" asks Soares.

"More than ever!" Daniel replies.

"Good! Very good!" approves Soares. "I believe you will do well. But now we have a long trip ahead of us. Why don't you go below and try to get some sleep?"

Shortly after seven o'clock that evening, the whalers row their boats to shore in Lajes. A few of the townspeople have gathered to watch the boats come in and to hear the news. One of the men in the town's band gives Francisco's crew a hand as the men haul their boat back up into the whale boat shed.

Daniel and the *Cigana* do not arrive until midnight.

In the morning, Daniel gets up early. He is eager to get a close look at the whales caught the day before. When he reaches the whale processing factory at the edge of town, he finds that men are already swarming over the huge whale carcasses.

One team of men are busy flensing —stripping the blubber from the whale's body with cutting spades. The fat comes off in long, curling, thick white sheets, which are chopped into large squares. Other men haul them off with grappling poles to the boiling vats, where the blubber is melted down into oil.

In former times, the fine oil that comes from sperm whales was used in the manufacture of soaps, perfumes, margarine, lubricants for machinery, and fuel for lamps. Today, the oil is used mainly for the making of better quality soaps.

Another team of men are hacking away at the carcass of the other whale, from which most of the blubber has been removed. Nothing is wasted. The whale's meat and bones are chopped up, dried, and ground into fertilizer— *boana.* Even the blood is dried and used for fertilizer.

The whalers will receive their share of the profits at the end of the whaling season, when all of the oil has been sold. The money from the sale of the whale fertilizer will all go to the processing factory. If it is a good season, Francisco will earn three or four thousand escudos from whaling.

Back at the house everyone is in a gay mood. Today is the second day of the *festas,* and there are still three more days to look forward to. This week no one will work very much. Unless, of course, whales are sighted again!

Daniel and his family walk to the *festa* in the village of Ribeira do Meio, a few miles up the coast. People from all over Pico have come to this tiny community, and there are even some visitors from neighboring islands.

Although today's *festa* has religious significance, it is also a joyful occasion. For almost a week, the women who can afford it have been baking the special, costly vesper bread. Now they march triumphantly down the main road in two long lines. On their heads they carry huge baskets of bread and flowers —symbols of the miracle granted to Queen Isabel. The women are bringing the bread to the church in the village square to be blessed by the priest. As always, at the front of their procession walks a little girl. She represents Queen Isabel and carries a large silver replica of her crown.

65

Maria do Egipto wants to go into the church to light a candle for her father's soul, but it is impossible. Almost every inch of the church's floor is covered by the large baskets of bread. Even the sidewalks of the square are heaped with the lovely baskets. The fragrance of bread and flowers fills the air.

A priest comes out of the church. A man walks beside him carrying a silver cup of holy water. The priest sprinkles the water on the baskets saying, "I bless this bread in the sainted memory of Good Queen Isabel and in the name of the Father, the Son, and the Holy Spirit. Amen."

Down the street, the giving of the bread begins. Everyone who attends the *festas* will receive a loaf of vesper bread—the young and the old, the rich and the poor alike.

On a wooden platform next to the church, the members of the band from Lajes take their places. They make a handsome sight in their smart uniforms. Daniel's brother is the band's drummer. At the bandmaster's signal, José Manuel rolls off a flourish on his drum and the band strikes up the national anthem of Portugal.

Daniel scrambles up the rear of the platform to stand next to his brother. Then he begins to stamp his foot in time to the music. The people at the front of the crowd start cheering Daniel's performance, but José Manuel becomes embarrassed.

"Get off, you little fool!" he hisses at his brother. "What are you trying to do to me?"

"I was just trying to help you out," says Daniel mischievously. He jumps down from the platform and vanishes into the crowd.

In a narrow lane of the village, a small group of men have begun the dance of the bread and the wine. They seem to have had much more wine than bread, thinks Daniel as he wanders by, but he admires their enthusiasm. So do the other onlookers.

The band finishes its concert and the family rejoins. They decide to visit a nearby village called Prainha, where another *festa* is taking place today. They will receive their vesper bread there.

In the village square they are given loaves that look like large doughnuts. This is the traditional shape of the vesper bread of Prainha.

Daniel wanders off toward the edge of the village near the shoreline. A group of boys are setting off fireworks and small rockets. Daniel remembers the sound of the whaling rockets. Was it only yesterday that he heard them? It seems hard to believe now.

After the excitement of the *festas*, life once more resumes its normal pace for the people of Lajes. The fields must be tended. Fresh *bolo* must be baked. And the men of Pico must go out to sea to hunt the whales.

José Vigario has given Daniel one of the teeth of the first whale killed on that first day's hunt. In his spare time, Daniel has been practicing the art of scrimshaw — engraving on whale teeth. The New Bedford whalers introduced this craft to the Azores in the nineteenth century.

With a thin, pointed tool, Daniel has engraved a drawing of a sperm whale on the whale tooth. Next he rubs india ink over the tooth until it has seeped into all the lines of the engraving. When he removes the excess ink with a rag, a black engraving remains. He will treasure this memento of his first whale hunt for a long time.

Daniel has heard that in some parts of the world, men hunt whales from great ships and shoot at the animals with powerful guns. How, he wonders, can this equal the thrill or the challenge of personal combat between man and beast? No, he decides, as long as there are whales in the sea and men of Pico to hunt them, he will follow their way. One day, he too will become a whale hunter of Pico.

914.69
WOL
    Wolf, Bernard
        Daniel and the
        whale hunters

8272

914.69
WOL
    Wolf, Bernard
        Daniel and the
        whale hunters

8272

DATE DUE	BORROWER'S NAME	
16 '77	Thomas Luong	138